Create, Expand and Retain Your Customers

The B2B Solution for Increasing Your Bottom Line and Edging out Your Competitors

By Robin Black

Published: November 2013

®Connects Marketing Group

Special Thanks

I feel blessed every day knowing that I get to work with some of the best people to walk this planet. Our clients new and old have taught us so much. It is a pleasure growing with them.

It is hard to know where to start to thank those who have given me direction, guidance, love and support over the years.

Lisa Schulte has been my close friend, manager and right hand for the last 15 years. I love you, friend! My friends and staff have stayed the course with me through the slow times and the crazy busy times. Thank you Bev Monte Calvo, Gretchen Cole, Andrea Estrada, DeDe Campbell, Aristana Firethorne, Rachel DaSilva and Joanne Wagner. Words cannot express how much you all mean to me. Christine Mulcahy has helped with her amazing talent for internal and customer-facing presentations. Wendy Sack, our writer extraordinaire, without her, this book and our blogs would never have happened.

Special thanks to my daughter, Jessica Manca; I love you to the moon and back. To my sister, Bonnie Gruger, the one person who has been there for me my entire life- I love you, sister. Last but never least, the love of my life, my husband, Tim Callison, who taught me that life is indeed perfect.

Dedication

This book is dedicated to my clients, current and future. Thank you for your continued support, for the opportunity to help you grow your businesses and all that you have taught me in return.

Table of Contents

Introduction	6
Connects Marketing Group: Perfecting the Art of Business Development	7
What Is the True Cost of a Lead? (Probably Not What You Thought)	22
The Connects Component: Turning Leads into Customers	40
Maximizing Your Return on Investment (ROI)	50
Creating Customers: Building Your Lead Generation Machine	52
Expanding Customers: Mining the Gold in Your Top Customers	57
Retaining Customers: Keeping Them Profitable for the Long Term	60
Other Core Competencies: Tools to Make Your Business Hum	63
Reporting: The Feedback Loop to Refine Your Efforts	66
Case Studies: How It Works in the Real World	68
Testimonials: What Our Clients Think	71
Conclusion	73
Helpful Resources: Industry-Leading Blogs	74
About the Author	75

Introduction

At Connects Marketing Group, we are experts in helping our B2B clients create, retain and expand their customers.

In this book we'll talk a bit about our company and a lot about the proven methodologies you can use to increase your bottom line and edge out your competitors.

Whether you're reading this in your garage or your corner office, are a start-up or a Fortune 500 OEM, these are the cutting-edge techniques that can make the difference between merely surviving and growing into the leader in your industry.

You'll learn how to determine the true cost of a qualified sales-ready lead and be able to calculate the return on investment for all of your outbound and inbound marketing initiatives.

Then you'll find out how you can use the Connects Component to not only find and create new customers, but also keep your current ones loyal and grow them exponentially to exceed what you ever thought possible.

In the end, it always comes down to connections- reaching the decision-makers, nurturing relationships and going beyond what you thought you knew about sales.

Connections Matter.

"Marketing is anything and everything one can do to cause new business to happen with the right people at the right time."

Connects Marketing Group: Perfecting the Art of Business Development

When it comes to new business, Connections Matter. At Connects Marketing Group, we recognize there is an art to having business development conversations with new prospects and existing customers. We do more than B2B lead generation for our clients. We partner with them to identify new business opportunities and establish high-quality relationships that start strong, stay vital and evolve into long-term alliances.

We are committed to personalizing, customizing and humanizing B2B lead generation, business development and sales program management for our clients. Our people and their attitudes are one of our greatest strengths. A seasoned team of naturally curious and enthusiastic professionals, we are committed to your success and filling your pipeline with highly-qualified business opportunities.

It's all in the connections we will make for you.

In a nutshell

Connects is a B2B marketing company specializing in clients of any size and in any vertical - from small start-ups to Fortune 500 OEMs, low- to high-tech.

Our specialties are customer creation, lead generation and nurturing, market research and creation and business strategy. We help you create, expand and retain your customers.

Our mission is simple:

Our first goal is to have a deep and comprehensive knowledge of your company, your culture, your programs and your products.

Our ultimate goal is to fill your pipeline with well-qualified leads and the details needed to ensure a smooth execution by your sales team.

We are:
Quality conversationalists committed to personalizing, customizing and humanizing the activity of lead generation and business development with your existing clients and new prospects.

We are:
A woman-owned, results-focused, B2B marketing company with a track record of successfully selling complex and technical products and solutions at all levels of an enterprise.

Two things set Connects Marketing Group apart from the rest.

1. The quality of our staff is unmatched.

The most important aspect of a B2B company's marketing program, especially in today's digital marketplace, is the people delivering the message. The human component is an unquantifiable element of greatest priority because it is in the chemistry between those delivering a company's message and the potential customers where the relationships are developed- or lost. Because real people make business decisions on the customer end, every point of contact you have with them makes or breaks the potential connections you stand to create.

Although the bulk of what we do involves calling, please don't call us telemarketers. That word doesn't even begin to scratch the surface of what we do for you. We are customer creation, expansion and retention professionals. We don't replace your sales and marketing teams, we **complement** them.

Our greatest asset is our team of individuals, each of whom uses a variety of approaches to best interpret the messages your company wishes to convey, through both spoken and written communication. With our proven system of streamlined strategies and our competent, professional and extensively skilled team, we can immediately mobilize our efforts to collaborate with your company and get valuable results beyond what you might expect using your own people, who could be preoccupied in other areas besides those in which we specialize.

Most importantly, each member of our team possesses an **extensive sales and technical background**. In fact, it is not uncommon for clients to seek out sales or technical advice from their Connects project manager or callers. Each of us is fully qualified and beyond capable of working shoulder-to-shoulder with your top sales people, assisting them in identifying and overcoming pain points in the sales cycle, providing strategic advice, services and tools that will lead to, for example, better competitive positioning, a consistently-filled, qualified sales pipeline, shorter sales cycles and more importantly, market leadership, increased revenue and reduced costs. As a group, we help monitor your business strategy, modify where necessary and help you stay on track to achieve your goals.

We work in highly technical and complicated B2B industries, from software and computer technology to medical devices and the financial industry and with all levels within each organization, including R&D, engineering, marketing and sales. We couldn't make it in these industries without the sales and technical experience to fall back on, and we have both in spades.

Our Clients' Industries Include:

- Aerospace
- Automotive
- Computer Technology & Software
- Medical Devices
- Industrial
- Financial Coaching
- Fluid Power/Hydraulics
- Components
- Alternative Energies
- Food & Beverage

Here's an example of the work we're doing with one of our current clients.

Client: Global seal manufacturer

Project: Mapping of a current customer

Results: First 15 hours resulted in an opportunity worth $200k-$300k.

Many other projects were unearthed in previously untapped divisions within the customer's organization.

Project in Review
5/1/2013 – 6/3/2013

Hours	Calls	CPH	Pres.	PPH	Pres.%	Leads	Lead %	Cost
100	503	5.0	105	1.1	21%	37	35%	$162

Hot	Warm	Pending	Lit Only	No Interest	Referral	Bad Data
18	19	1	6	40	22	25
17%	18%	1%	6%	38%	21%	N/A

Comments: We have successfully qualified 37 leads. Seven people requested additional information. We obtained 22 new referrals which we will be following up with. 40 of the 105 people we spoke with did not have interest (more details below).

While more and more purchasing decisions are in fact being made online, your customers and prospects should have a real-live person, face-to-face or over the phone, to discuss their particular needs. This is especially true in most B2B scenarios, where complex engineering or technical situations are critical.

For instance, an engineer designing an aircraft engine isn't going to spec in your part simply because he interacts with your company online. He should have a good feel (read: brand awareness) for your company, and hopefully have been given all of the technical information he might have needed, but at the end of the day, he's going to want to speak with an actual person, probably R&D and sales, to get to the meat of his product needs. The same is true for a vast array of highly technical, engineering-based industries.

That's where the good, old-fashioned personal interaction is always going to be needed. Personal contact is key to ensuring a successful outcome for all involved, and Connects works seamlessly with your sales and marketing team to make this happen.

2. We are unbelievable conversationalists.

Our callers are unbelievable conversationalists. We know how to get people relaxed so they will be comfortable and share information with us. An important key to that is active listening. This allows us to provide your sales engineers with a virtual welcome mat at the front door of a prospective client.

Each employee of Connects was hand-picked and has been nurtured and grown into a part of our team. From a management standpoint, I handle employees just as Connects handles your customers. The right people become the best colleagues and develop into the best team. That's what we have at Connects. Our team is unmatched in knowledge, professionalism and passion. We know what our clients want and how to get it for them- and we love our jobs!

Think of having your dream job, where you love to go to work each day and get excited about the outcomes that you create. That's what each of our callers brings to your table. A sense of ownership of each project drives us to do our best for all of our clients, and this starts with creating career-long connections with your prospects and customers.

If you're a sales professional reading this, imagine having the time to truly cultivate and nurture each and every prospect or customer in your territory. You're dreaming, right? There aren't enough hours in the day to do that plus all of your additional tasks. That missing piece- THAT is what Connects callers do for you. We nurture your targets, accelerating the speed of trust, and forge relationships that translate into satisfied customers.

We believe B2B lead generation should be about the **Three C's: Contact, Communication and Connections.** They are the foundation of our success. They matter. We do them right, each and every time.

We take our role in your sales development process very personally. We excel in cultivating transparency and trust with every communication between our clients, their teams and their customers.

- We thrive on challenges.
- We absolutely live to excel.
- We believe in being both high touch and high tech.
- We uncover the best possible customers for our clients.
- We take communicating with clarity and authenticity seriously.
- We believe in making each exchange both effective and memorable.
- We make the sales team look great before they arrive for their first meeting.
- We have fun doing it.

Each touch point of communication is an opportunity to create a deeper connection, uncover more opportunities to be of service, share information, offer solutions and enrich a working relationship while moving through the customer's decision-making journey.

"Robin Black and her team have made a huge contribution in accelerating our success over the last two years. They have earned our total confidence so that we now entrust their team to be the first to engage every one of the many prospective client that comes to us each week. They have proven to be an invaluable partner in all components of both our businesses; CEG Worldwide and Financial Advisor Select."
John Bowen, CEO, CEG Worldwide and Financial Advisor Select

How we connect...

What we connect...

The human element

Companies today are expending huge amounts of energy creating content and marketing in the digital space. We believe that digital media is very passive. The content is great, but really puts the onus on your customers and prospects to find the information that is most valuable to them.

Your marketing is effective. Your digital footprint exists. We are your company's human element. Through intensive training, we become virtual employees of our clients'- speaking to prospects as a seamless extension of your company.

By using the human approach, we can reach the people who really need to hear your message.

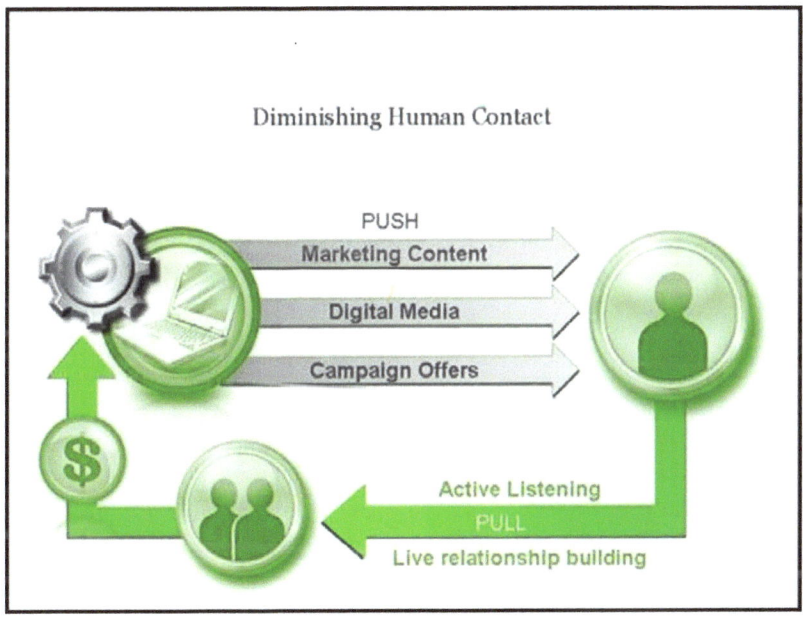

Why wouldn't I just use my in-house sales and marketing team?

You invest a great deal in your sales professionals. The best place for them to be is in front of decision-makers, closing deals. By using Connects, you make that possible.

Utilizing Connects helps your in-house team focus only on highly qualified closeable leads. We help with the day-to-day digging so they can put more time and energy into making the sales. Because we have so much experience, putting us to work for you means you don't have to train new employees; we can learn your project and be ready to go within two weeks.

We don't stop with the initial training. As your project progresses, we bring what we've learned to the table and fine-tune our messaging as we go along, incorporating new products or services as desired.

We are experts in our field and become experts in yours as well. This is what we do. We focus on establishing and sustaining relationships with your customers so your sales team can focus on closing deals. We're telemarketers on steroids – we cold-call, qualify and nurture leads and provide solid metrics to support your marketing and sales efforts, devoting our expertise to building your pipeline so you don't have to.

Immediate Feedback Loop

We are extremely tech-savvy. It is not uncommon for Connects project managers and callers to give advice to clients on how best to use the clients' business management software. If there's a system you use that we haven't, we can learn it.

One of the most valuable aspects of our service is the continuous feedback. Because we leverage all current technologies, such as Salesforce.com, Time-Trade, Mind-Jet and Docu-Sign, to name a few, we are able to provide almost daily results. We can tell you what's working, what needs to be tweaked and what your prospects are saying. The data we capture is incredibly granular and the metrics and analytics can be sliced and diced and reported back to you in myriad formats. At any given time, any report you request is available.

Our feedback is virtually live and is something that you don't get from more traditional forms of marketing such as trade shows, advertising or industry product and supplier sourcing platforms, even social media.

Know your audience

Your customers and prospects are individuals. Just as any salesperson worth his or her salt knows, your pitch has to be tailored to your audience.

Our team applies SolutionPeople's 4-quadrant 4Brain Thinkers Model™ to our methodologies. This means that while on the phone with your prospects, our callers can determine to what type of personality they are speaking and fine-tune your message to be most effective.
We can get a feel for the kind of person we're speaking with and steer our conversations to meet his or her needs. This involves more than simply knowing someone's job title. It ties back into actively listening to understand how a person's brain really works.

Four Quadrants

Conversation barriers
↗ Product vs. solution selling
↗ Role-based business pains
↗ Personality types

Conversation solutions
↗ Positioning and messaging frameworks
↗ Discussing business and technical requirements
↗ Adjusting the conversation based on customer's dominant brain type

More on the Four Quadrants

Investigator:
Seeks information, data or understanding of a problem
Provide them with as much data as possible
They need to process data before they can begin to think about a possible idea

Creator:
Comes up with ideas
Only wants to hear the top level ideas
They want to hear ideas up front and get excited

Evaluator:
Decides if the idea will be a solution
Wants to know what kind of criteria is being
They want to know cause vs. effect, pros vs. cons, etc.

Activator:
Puts the solution into practice
Wants to know how easy it will be to implement
They want to know what resources are involved, etc.

Depending on what brain type your listener has, sales pitches, presentations and conversations can be adapted in order to more effectively communicate.

The bottom line: At Connects Marketing Group we approach your prospects and clients as we would want to be approached ourselves. We talk, but most importantly, we listen.

What Is the True Cost of a Lead? (Probably Not What You Thought)

The true cost of a lead involves many layers of attention, all of which are critical.

- Creating a marketing approach and executing the strategy
- Devoting the time it takes to contact potential customers using all available means
- Diligently following up on and nurturing those leads

The time investment in business development cannot be underestimated, and as stated previously, most companies would rather have their sales staff's time and energy focused solely on closing deals and delivering products/services

The old adage is true: Time is Money. The more efficient your process is for developing customers, the higher the ROI on your marketing budget will be.

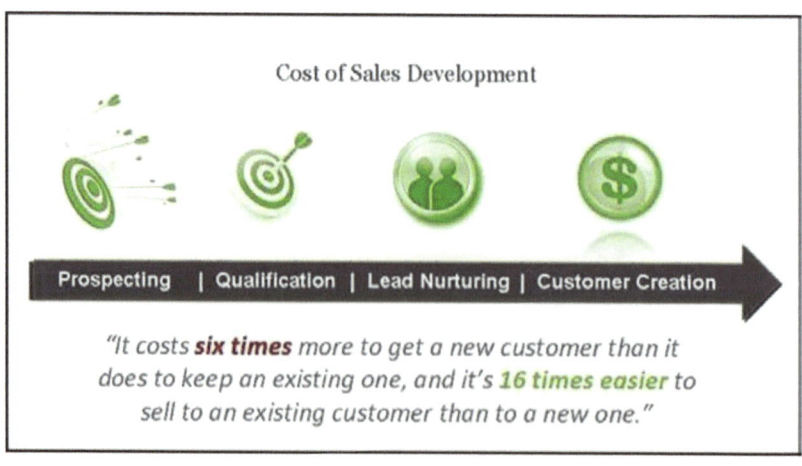

"It costs **six times** more to get a new customer than it does to keep an existing one, and it's **16 times easier** to sell to an existing customer than to a new one."

Let's take a look at some of the traditional sources of leads and how much they cost.

We'll use the old tried and true formula for ROI:

(Gross Profit - Marketing Expenses) / Marketing Expenses

Then we'll use the following for cost per lead:

Total Spent/ Number of Leads Generated

Trade Shows

We'll start with the beast in all marketing budgets: the trade show. Now, depending on the size of your company and the money you have to spend, the size of your booth will vary.

For this, we'll consider a 30 x 40 space at Process Expo 2013. That puts our price per square foot at about $32, including drayage. We'll also assume that you have an existing booth, so our estimate excludes a new custom booth build or rental. However, according to the Exhibit Designers and Producers Association's 2011 Economic Survey, current custom exhibit costs range from $144 to $160 per square foot.

Image Credit: soazcai.org

23

Item	Expense
Booth Space	$38,400
Show Services (all site costs minus carpenter)	$20,000
Labor*	$2,387
Flights & Travel	$20,000
Car Rentals	$2,000
Hotels & Accommodations	$12,000
Promo Items	$5,000
Customer Entertainment	$15,000
Food/ Other	$20,000
Total	$134,787

*Some companies choose to use their own Install & Dismantle companies; however, certain tasks, depending on city, can only be performed by Union labor. For this calculation, we are only considering general Union carpentry. Union electrician, rigger and forklift not included. Chicago average is $119.35/hr. We'll consider two Union carpenters for 10 hours each on regular time.
Source: Red7Media's Trade Show Labor Rate Benchmarking Survey

Knowing that the B2B sales cycle can be quite lengthy, it will take a few weeks or months before you know for sure what your gross profit was from the Process Expo. For our purposes, let's say you had a gross profit of $200,000 with 98
leads generated. Remember that gross profit only includes sales that happened as a <u>direct result</u> of your company's attendance at the Expo.

ROI (200,000 – 134,787) / 134,787= 48.3%
Cost per Lead 137,787/ 98= $1,375.38

Wow! An ROI of 48.3% is amazing! But wait. Is that your true ROI? And a cost per lead of almost $1,400! Let's back this truck up.

The one crucial piece of the puzzle missing here is this: **how many of these leads were qualified, sales-ready leads?** And how many were garbage? According to multiple industry resources, anywhere from 5% to 30% of your leads from a given trade show are qualified. Meaning that's the percentage of leads that have full contact information and application needs, etc.

So for argument's sake, we'll say that 30% of your leads from the above show were qualified. That translates to about 29 leads that can be handed off to your sales people right out of the gate. If your sales people have time to jump right on these leads, that is.

The stats below are from the Center for Exhibition Industry Research (CEIR), particularly, their [Exhibitor Sales Lead Capture and Follow-up Practice Trends](#) research report released in October 2012.

> *The top two most common methods organizations use to capture leads are: lead retrieval system offered by an exhibition organizer, 74 percent, and paper-based lead form/collect business cards, 59 percent.*
>
> *Qualifying leads is infrequent, with only 30 percent of exhibitors capturing demographics and other lead qualifier questions, in addition to contact information and product or service interest information.*
>
> *Customized emails, 64 percent, and phone follow-up tailored to address attendee product or service interests, 59 percent, are the most common follow-up methods. Fulfillment of these efforts is completed within two weeks by over 70 percent of exhibitors using each method.*

The point is this: pre- and post- show connections are a vital part of trade show lead generation success. This includes comprehensive marketing tactics to bring traffic to your booth in the first place. Even if you come out with 29 "qualified leads," those prospects still need further qualification before they're ready to be handed off to your sales people. To say nothing of the other 67 leads, which deserve to be vetted as well. When all is said and done, your ROI is going to be driven down and your cost per lead driven up.

B2B companies are allocating 12% of their budget to trade shows but only getting 9% of their leads from that source. (Source: HubSpot)

61% of B2B marketers say that generating high-quality leads is their biggest challenge. (Source: B2B Lead Generation Marketing Trends Survey 2013)

Virtual Trade Shows

Virtual trade shows are becoming more and more popular in the B2B world, with marketers exhausted with spending so much money on traditional shows and struggling to prove their effectiveness.

Here are some of the pros and cons if you're considering a virtual event.

Pros
- No travel costs
- No hotel/accommodation costs
- No booth costs
- You can "exhibit" at, or sponsor, many more shows- more economically feasible (Hosting the show will be more expensive, of course)
- You can reach a bigger audience
- You automatically get contact information from any prospect who clicks on your "booth"

Cons
- Limited networking opportunities, because your sales people aren't walking the show hall
- Can't "see" or "touch" products

- Could have a more social feel; less serious business discussions
- Excludes those who are not tech savvy
- Sales people, engineers, etc. still have to spend hours or days away from their usual tasks

The point is this: Virtual trade shows are substantially more affordable than traditional ones, especially for smaller companies. They also usually last longer and can produce a large number of prospects. While you pay less for these prospects, they're still not qualified. The same thing we said about traditional shows applies here. Pre- and post-show connections and marketing are necessary, meaning that while your ROI and cost-per-lead for these events are usually better in the virtual world, getting to fully qualified leads ready for hand-off will drive those factors down and up, respectively.

Print Advertising

How many times have you had the "print is dead" debate with other marketing colleagues? If you're like me, it's more times than you care to count. Yes, there is something to be said for branding. The truth is, though, that your audience is increasingly moving online.

From Marketo:
Advertisers knew this trend was coming as more and more people started moving towards the online world. A recent report released by eMarketer earlier this year states that 2012 would be the year that spending for online advertising would surpass spending for print advertising. In 2011, online ad spending grew 23% in the US, just passing the $32 billion mark, and in 2012 the online ads will grow another 23% to nearly $40 billion. As the spending for online ads continues to grow, B2B marketing professionals need to watch for this development and catch on quickly because we live in an increasingly interactive world, and opportunities to market to your future customers could be lost if this is ignored.

As with anything in branding, the key to advertising is having a consistent presence. That's hard to do in print if you don't have a limitless budget. As an example, below is the 2013 rate schedule for one of the number one trade magazines in B2B manufacturing. (Source: *Machine Design*)

PRINT & DIGITAL REACH..134,000

MONTHLY ONLINE REACH...175,000

MONTHLY E-NEWSLETTER REACH............................90,500

Display Rates

B&W	1X	12X	Color	Per Page	Per Spread
Full Page	$10,700	$9,915	Standard Process	$1,390	$2,200
2/3 Page	$8,020	$7,430	Matched Color	$2,745	$4,390
Island Half	$7,695	$7,025	3 & 4 Color Process	$2,745	$4,390
1/2 Page	$6,110	$5,660	5 Color	$4,760	$7,600
1/3 Page	$4,295	$3,980	Bleed	No Charge	No Charge
1/4 Page	$3,150	$2,990			
Data File	$1,410				

Let's say you wanted to run one full-page ad per month in this trade magazine. Per your company's brand standards, you are required to use at least a 4-color process. That puts your total spend at $42,855 for the year.

Now, for the sake of this example, let's say you receive 50 inquiries per month based on your ads. We're only going to calculate cost per lead, since the ROI on print advertising is so subjective.

Item	Expense
One full-page ad per month	$9,915
4-color process ($2,745 per ad)	$32,940
Total	$42,855

Circulation (print and digital) of 134,000, so impressions are likely to be high. This is not something that is easily measured for ROI.
For this exercise, we will use the number of inquiries per ad. We'll say 50 per month.

Cost per Lead 42,855/ 600= $71.43

Stop the presses! (Pun definitely intended) That is an outstanding cost per lead. But let's be real. Based on real-life experience, we know that 50 inquiries per month on a print ad is a bit high. Doable, but high. The bigger problem is the quality of these inquiries. After qualification, your number will probably drop to somewhere within the 5-10 real, quality leads per month.

This is more realistic (minus the cost for qualification)

Cost per Lead 42,855/ 120= $357.13

The point is this: Yes, you can calculate ROI and cost per lead for print advertising, but it's a bit tricky. Your ads need to contain some sort of call to action so that you can track clicks on a specified web page, or something similar. But even then, these are only prospects. They still need to be qualified.

Email Marketing

Email marketing has come a very long way since the days of simply pumping out mass messages from your company's CRM system and praying that your targets will open them. There are some very sophisticated email-marketing providers out there that are really doing it right. Constant Contact is one that most everyone knows.

In researching email-marketing statistics, I came across these from Jay Baer over at ConvinceandConvert.com. These statistics were gathered through email subscriber studies.

- **21%** of email recipients report email as Spam, even if they know it isn't
- **43%** of email recipients click the Spam button based on the email "from" name or email address
- **69%** of email recipients report email as Spam based solely on the subject line
- **35%** of email recipients open email based on the subject line alone
- IP addresses appearing on just one of the **12** major blacklists had email deliverability **25** points below those not listed on any blacklists
- Email lists with **10%** or more unknown users get only 44% of their email delivered by ISPs
- **17%** of Americans create a new email address every 6 months
- **30%** of subscribers change email addresses annually
- If marketers optimized their emails for image blocking, ROI would increase **9+%**
- **84%** of people 18-34 use an email preview pane
- People who buy products marketed through email spend **138%** more than people that do not receive email offers
- **44%** of email recipients made at least one purchase last year based on a promotional email
- Subscribers below age **25** prefer SMS to email
- **35%** of business professionals check email on a mobile device
- **80%** of social network members have received unsolicited email or invites

The point is this: 75% of marketers say that they are using more email than they were three years ago. (Source: HubSpot) Building a quality email distribution list takes a major time investment. It can be an excellent way to share information with your prospects and customers, but gathering qualified leads from email marketing still takes that extra step of connection.

Of all the types of traditional marketing we just covered, they all have one thing in common: They do not stand alone. There is still a layer of connection that needs to happen to produce quality, qualified, sales-ready leads. We'll call that the Connects Component. We'll discuss it in more detail in a little bit. First, let's take a look at inbound marketing.

Inbound Marketing

Everyone knows how expensive traditional (outbound) marketing can be. Generating leads through activities such as trade shows and advertising is a tried and true approach; however, the times they are a 'changin. There has been a monumental shift towards online (inbound) marketing over the past few years, with companies believing that this will be an easy and inexpensive route.

> "Audiences everywhere are tough. They don't have time to be bored or brow beaten by orthodox, old-fashioned advertising. We need to stop interrupting what people are interested in and be what people are interested in." ***Craig Davis, CCO Worldwide, J. Walter Thompson (world's fourth largest ad agency)***

What is inbound marketing?

Inbound marketing is the process of creating quality online content that draws your target audience to your company, where you can convert them to loyal customers over time.

This is a 180 from traditional outbound marketing, such as trade shows, print advertising and email blasts.

Inbound Marketing Methodology

- Inbound marketing is not a tactic, channel, or technology. It's a way to approach to your marketing to capitalize on the way consumers make buying decisions today.
- Inbound marketers understand that people value personalized, relevant content and connections -- not interruptive messages -- at every stage of the marketing funnel.
- Inbound allows you to attract visitors, convert leads, close customers, and delight them into promoting your business to others.

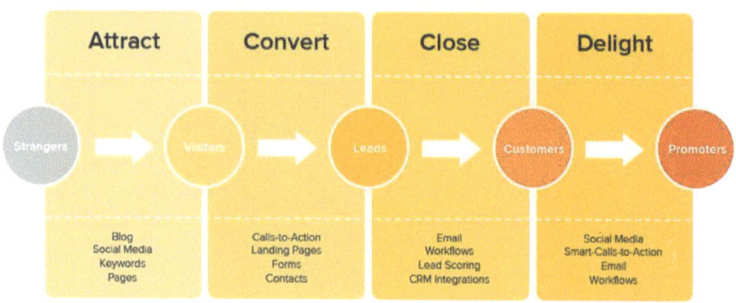

Here are the top 10 insights from HubSpot's 2013 State of Inbound Marketing Annual Report:

- **Inbound Marketing's Rise**: Nearly 60% practice inbound.
- **Stronger ROI Than Traditional**: Twice as many marketers see below-average leads via inbound
- **Traditional Is Fading**: Inbound grew around 50% for the third straight year.
- **Definition and Data**: Some marketers still struggle with defining and analyzing inbound.
- **Capturing a Difficult Audience**: Inbound cuts through the cluttered internet to reach consumers at every stage of their buying decisions.
- **Smarter Marketing**: Automation of certain tactics allows marketers to focus on newer tasks like blogging.
- **Inbound Means Marketing**: Successful marketers grasp that inbound is not a channel or a technology but a strategy.
- **Consumers Win**: Inbound creates marketing people love because it adds value at every stage.
- **Marketers Win, Too**: No longer cost centers to companies or nuisances to consumers, marketers are more lovable (and important) than ever.
- **Content And Context**: Content is just part of the equation. Context systems like CRMs are still needed to personalize the buyer journey and drive real ROI.

From the same survey:

Inbound Marketing Improves Lead Acquisition Margins

Inbound vs. Traditional

Do you do inbound marketing?	Average Cost per Lead	Average Cost per Customer
Yes	$36	$254
No	$41	$268

Survey N =3,339

B2B Cost per Lead 53% Higher Than B2C Companies

Sales Channel	Average Cost per Lead	Average Cost per Customer
B2B	$43	$264
B2C	$15	$149

Survey Segment N =1,917

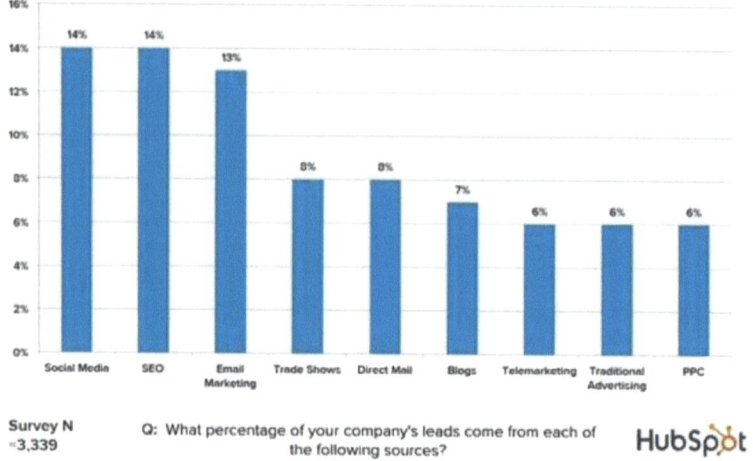

Inbound marketing is definitely where it's at. It outperforms outbound in most categories. But alas, there is no such thing as free marketing.

So many marketers get swept up into the social media and content creation wave, thinking they've found the golden ticket- the loophole that will allow them to market like the big boys, but on a shoestring budget. Companies should be completely honest with themselves about the true costs of these activities.

In considering inbound marketing, there are two aspects that warrant special attention: the cost of content creation and actual online traffic numbers.

1. Marketers underestimate the cost of quality content creation

What is content creation?

Simply, content creation is the consistent creation of useful, thoughtful and informative content. Examples are blogs, websites, e-learning courses, social media channels or mobile apps.

The goal of content creation is to engage your brand with prospects and customers on every step of the buying journey- from initial introduction to the transition into your biggest fan.

To say that content creation is low-cost or even free is like crafting your marketing budget wearing blinders. Quality content creation is anything but free, especially if you're working in highly technical industries where your goal is to share knowledge and provide value to your customers. And really, no matter the industry, shouldn't that always be the goal in our B2B world?

Let's take a real-life example. You're tasked with content creation for a company that engineers and manufactures safety-critical components for the aerospace industry. Where are you going to find your technical experts?

Internal Subject Matter Experts are Not Free Labor

Let's say you're going to start with your internal product engineers as well as your research and development department. Depending on the complexity of the product, service or application you'd like to discuss, your subject matter experts (SMEs) will need to spend a certain amount of time for the creation of these materials.

Since you want a consistent flow of information, developing these materials, be they presentations, video or web tutorials, white papers or online training courses, you're looking at a large number of hours per SME. Remember, you also have to allow for any reviewing and editing cycles that will need to occur before the materials can be released.

Consider this:

- Your organization's target is 75 online training courses per year.

- For each course, 50 hours of your SMEs' time is required.

- Your SMEs each make $130,000 per year.

- That puts your cost per hour at $63 per hour.

- Your annual cost would then be $236,000.

In this scenario, you'll also want to take into account that each SME will be taken away from his or her daily activities to create content for the organization, meaning a loss of productivity in their respective departments.

External Vendors are Not Your Employees

Of course you can always outsource your content creation to an external vendor, but you need to be very careful in this situation. A key element to your content creation strategy should be original content, and for that you'll pay an outside resource a premium. After all, you'll need someone who is not only tech savvy, but knowledgeable in applicable engineering.

Industry knowledge will be your main concern, but you'll also need to be aware of and be able to review for any plagiarized content.

In other words, you want to be sure that your outside vendor isn't picking pieces of content up from other sources and trying to pass it off as original content for your organization. Not only could that be a legal nightmare, it could also tarnish your reputation in the industry.

Now I'm not saying that all outside vendors are unreliable. Not at all! That would be shooting myself in the foot. What I'm saying is that whenever you entrust your company's voice to someone who isn't invested in its success, a higher level of scrutiny is always called for.

Website Infrastructure

One more aspect to consider is the cost of implementing your website's infrastructure. If you are hosting your own e-learning or customer area for online tools, you'll need to factor in the cost for these activities.

Those costs include the actual development of these tools themselves, not just the technical content that will drive them. Quality programming and maintenance are important elements for any website tools.

2. Your online traffic is probably inflated

In the realm of inbound marketing, businesses pay top dollar for search engine optimization (SEO) and pay-per-click (PPC) campaigns. Depending on the competitiveness of your industry, the search engine top spot of a highly desired key word can all but deplete your entire PPC budget.

The real kicker in these types of campaigns is click fraud. Click fraud involves bogus clicks. In other words, you're paying for clicks that are generated by automatic click software, referred to as "bots," or human fraud.

Google states on its website that "On average, invalid clicks account for less than 10% of all clicks on AdWords ads." While 10 percent is relatively low compared to previous years, it can be too big of an ROI gamble for those companies with limited marketing dollars. More importantly, that 10 percent might not be accurate.

The biggest news to come out this year concerns the Chameleon botnet:

> *The discovery of the Chameleon botnet follows the recent takedown announcements of the Bamital botnet by Microsoft and Symantec—on February 6th of this year. Both the Chameleon botnet and the Bamital botnet have cost online advertisers millions of dollars. The Chameleon botnet is notable for the size of its financial impact: at a cost to advertisers of over 6 million dollars per month, it is at least 70 times more costly than the Bamital botnet. However, the Chameleon botnet is arguably even more notable for the fact that it is the first botnet found to be impacting display advertisers at scale (as opposed to text-link advertisers).*
>
> *(Source: spider.io)*

Some scary stats about the Chameleon botnet:

- **Date of discovery:** 28 February, 2013
- **Activity identified:** Botnet emulates human visitors on select websites causing billions of display ad impressions to be served to the botnet.
- **Number of host machines:** over 120,000 have been discovered so far
- **Proportion of traffic that is botnet traffic from IP addresses of host machines:** 90% (diluted by gateway IPs)
- **Number of target websites across which the botnet operates:** at least 202
- **Proportion of traffic across the target websites that is botnet traffic:** at least 65%
- **Number of ad impressions served to the botnet per month:** at least 9 billion
- **Number of distinct ad-exchange cookies associated with the botnet per month:** at least 7 million
- **Average click-through rate generated by the botnet:** 0.02%
- **Average mouse-movement rate generated by the botnet:** 11%
- **Average CPM paid by advertisers for ad impressions served to the botnet:** $0.69 CPM
- **Monthly cost to advertisers of ad impressions served to the botnet:** at least **$6.2 million**

In addition to click fraud, risks include content scraping and skimming. Basically, your content, hopefully ripe with key words, is stolen via old school copy/paste or high-tech software or programming and placed on another website, effectively diluting your SEO results. Think of it as digital-age plagiarism.

Inbound marketing is essential, but companies should be honest with themselves about the true costs of these activities.

The bottom line: Whether outbound or inbound, your marketing efforts should give you the most bang for your marketing buck. To make this happen, you must be honest with yourself about the true costs of a qualified lead.

The Connects Component: Turning Leads into Customers

So your company is fully immersed and engaged in its inbound marketing efforts. You've got all of your social media pages up and running, your blog is robust and updated in a timely fashion and your website is generating inbound leads like nobody's business because your SEO is on fire. You've hit the lead generation jackpot!

Now what? All of these leads still need to be qualified.

It's at this stage where most B2B companies falter. In the same way that in the past a pile of leads from a trade show would not be qualified and followed up on promptly, inbound marketing leads quickly become irrelevant if there is no system in place to convert them. If a prospect went online or to an event specifically to find you and you don't follow up in a timely manner, someone else is going to enjoy the business if you don't get back to them right away.

Some companies will put this task directly in the hands of sales engineers. Sales managers will say that they shouldn't have to pay for this, "that's what we pay our sales people for." They're right, but let's be honest. Sales engineers don't have time to follow up on all of these leads. Most sales engineers are consumed with day-to-day tasks and putting out fires, not looking for new business.

Prospects are actively seeking you out and still not actually reaching you.

Other companies will use some form of marketing automation to attempt to convert these unqualified leads into sales-ready opportunities. Marketing automation is a hot term these days. But what is it?

What is marketing automation?

Software solutions designed to simplify online processes by automating repetitive tasks. Automated marketing activities might include large-scale email marketing, lead scoring, ROI reporting, database de-duplication, file hosting, micro-level activity tracing for known and anonymous site visitors, drip nurturing and landing page building. (Source: Lead Lizard)

Marketing automation combines software with a company's CRM system and scores leads based on defined criteria. This information is supposed to allow the marketer to better target messages and promotions to individuals based on perceived interests. Marketing automation software can include email marketing, campaign management, lead nurturing/scoring, lead lifecycle management and analytics.

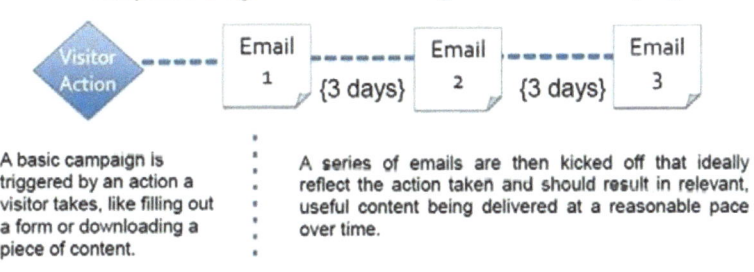

Simplified Diagram of a Marketing Automation Campaign

A basic campaign is triggered by an action a visitor takes, like filling out a form or downloading a piece of content.

A series of emails are then kicked off that ideally reflect the action taken and should result in relevant, useful content being delivered at a reasonable pace over time.

Source: HubSpot

Marketing automation is, in its most basic form, a tool with which to take inbound marketing leads and nurture them until they are ready to be converted to customers. While this can be somewhat helpful in the very beginning stages of a lead, letting your prospect know that you are aware of his or her interest and that you will be in contact, and that is where the automation should end.

At Connects Marketing Group, we believe that lead nurturing and conversion should be anything but automated. We believe that it is in this delicate stage, between the creation of a lead and the conversion of that lead to a customer, where you need someone, an actual person, who is dedicated to following up.

We'll call this the **Connects Component**.

Our Background

Company

- Leadership with experience implementing and managing projects for over 150 companies
- Proven track record of success
- Enjoy seeing our customers succeed and help exceed sales goals
- Vested interest in creating successful new business opportunities for your sales force

Personnel

- Relevant, direct experience in corporate environments
- Naturally curious, warm, approachable and trustworthy
- Skillful at establishing rapport, connection and agreement
- Ask relevant and impactful questions and actively listen to gather helpful details

The Connects component involves dedicated callers who are essentially an extension of your brand, who take pride in and ownership of the projects they are given. In other words, it is a true partnership, with your designated callers working earnestly towards your company's goals and objectives.

The Connects component means that you can nail the two most vital components of any successful marketing strategy:

1. **Reach your target audience with excellent ROI**
2. **Find out what's not working for your customers**

These two goals are achieved through a robust system of lead nurturing.

What is lead nurturing?

The term lead nurturing refers to a system for continuing a conversation with a prospect from initial contact until the prospect is sales-ready and/or the lead is closed and the business is lost or won.

Brian Carroll, founder and CEO of [InTouch](#) says, "Imagine your marketplace is like a field of banana trees. Your marketing people are those who nurture and pick the bananas. Bananas are harvested when they are green, and they turn yellow as they ripen. Fully 95 percent of your leads are like harvested green bananas, and, off the top, your sales team needs only the other 5 percent, those that are ripe."

Image Credit: act-on

Lead nurturing is all about connecting with your prospects. You need to find out what their needs are. What are the specifics of their applications? How can you help them achieve their goals? The most important part of this process is actively listening to what your customers and prospects are telling you.

Connects does this. You need unbelievable conversationalists, and that's what we are. We put a human element to all of the digital information that is already out there about your company.

With all the talk of marketing automation these days, you'd think that all companies have it together. This is not the case. There are so many organizations that simply have no system in place for following up on leads. That, or their sales people quite honestly do not have the time to do the follow up themselves.

Generating high-quality leads is a serious investment. Let's take a look at one real-world example.

> **Platform:** Website
>
> **Tool:** Online Member Area
>
> **Specifics:** In order to access etools, users are required to register their names, emails, locations and company names. They also have the option to give specific application or industry information.
>
> **Result:** Company has database of more than 20,000 members, broken down by date, location and whether or not theses members are current or prospective customers.
>
> **Costs:** Creation and implementation of etools (programming, etc.); time spent editing and monitoring content; web hosting
>
> It's hard to estimate the costs associated with web and etool creation, hosting, unless you talk about a specific company. It depends on the size of the company, the complexity of the site and tools, etc. For this particular real-world example, the company is a part of a multi-national corporation and offers complex etools and services targeted at engineers. An estimated budget for this could very well range into six figures.

Now ask yourself: if this situation existed in your company, how would you go about making sure that these leads were followed up on? Sure, you could set up some sort of automated system where anyone who signed up would receive an email and a kind of 'we are aware of your interest' letter.

But what if these leads require immediate action? Do your sales engineers have the resources and time to make that happen? More honestly, do they even care about these leads? Let's be blunt. A lot of sales engineers are territory-driven, so they don't want to spend their already stretched-thin time focusing on leads that won't affect them.

Enter the Connects Component:

Your new members are downloaded and contacted via phone within 24 hours of registration. Through a well-thought-out conversation based on a pre-determined set of questions, your inbound web leads are qualified (either in OR out) and turned into hot, actionable sales leads ready to be handed off to a sales engineer.

Listen folks, lead nurturing is so important in B2B sales that to not have a system in place is almost a criminal waste of marketing dollars. The sales pipeline for a B2B company is long and involved, and with employee turnover in play, it is vital to maintain a constant line of communication from inception to sale.

Connects makes that happen.

> "It is not uncommon for Connects callers to get return calls from targets one to two years after the completion of a project. That is, instead of picking up the phone and calling their sales engineer, customers become so engaged with us that we become their go-to people."
> **Gretchen Cole, Connects Project Manager**

We will get into specifics of ROI in the next sections, but let's talk about the other point:

What is NOT working for your customers?

That's right. As referenced previously, the second component to a successful marketing strategy is customer feedback. Leads that are qualified OUT are just as important as leads that are qualified IN and pushed along through the nurturing pipeline.

> "Failure is a strong word. It brings on visions of loss and defeat. In business, failure is just as important as success. Companies lose and gain market share all the times. It's a constant battle to be the best or have the best product. That's a good thing, competition means everyone has to be working hard to succeed. But for every winner, there are many losers. Failure is important because it helps companies and individuals to identify their weaknesses." ***Mike Fisher, examiner.com***

Any good CEO wants to know:

1. What do our customers think about us?

2. What is it about our company that disappoints you?

3. What can we do to improve?

4. Are our customers happy with our customer service?

5. What isn't working?

6. You might be asking yourself, "Can't I find that out with some sort of customer survey?" Well sure you can, but a good quality survey takes time and money and usually only happens once per calendar year. With the Connects process, you get instant customer feedback through daily reporting. This feedback is infinitely invaluable to a CEO and can help companies immediately put more dollars on the top line.

7. What products work in certain industries and not in others?

8. Are there product features that need to be adjusted?

9. Are there business practices that need to be improved or changed?

10. Are you happy with your level of service and support?

11. Which marketing tactics work and which don't?

12. Should you invest in that industry event?

13. Do you customers find your etools helpful?

14. Are there functionalities that would change that opinion?

Markets change so quickly. Your competitors often change their products and product positioning, so it can be difficult to keep track. There are too many things in terms of technology and methodologies impacting the market today, and economic struggles impacting your customers as well, to not invest in a daily customer feedback mechanism.

How We Measure Results

We value real-time reporting of metrics that matter. This allows for the team to adjust and continuously improve the process created for your project, assuring higher rates of success that much sooner. You will always be up to date on:

- Number of calls being made
- Number of connections established
- Number of highly qualified leads developed

Salespeople usually aren't frank enough to give you this kind of information. They tend to blame lost opportunities on products, be it price or features, while this may or may not be the case. The truth is that most sales engineers aren't trained to ask the right questions and actively listen to get this information from people.

Due to time constraints, most sales engineers unfortunately drop the ball when it comes to service and support after a deal is closed. Customer service is so, so important, and Connects does this for you.

Additionally, Connects callers <u>always</u> ask for referrals within the companies they are speaking with. Just because you qualify a person (e.g. R&D Manager) out, doesn't mean that you qualify a whole company out. Maybe you just haven't found the right person. Maybe the Principal Design Engineer has a hot project and needs you right away.

Connects finds these people for you.

> "Connects has been a terrific partner for doxo. They worked hard to really understand our unique value and benefits, and communicate very well to our prospects. We especially appreciate how proactive they are on measuring their results and iterating with us to improve our outcomes." **Steve Shrivers, CEO, doxo**

The bottom line: Think of the Connects Component as your secret weapon against your competitors. With your Connects team at work for you, you can be sure that you are getting the most from your hard-earned sales leads.

Maximizing Your Return on Investment (ROI)

The biggest factors in achieving successful ROI with Connects Marketing Group Process are:

Total buy-in from the organization, from the top down: From the President to the VP of Sales to the Marketing Manager and Sales Engineers, everyone has bought in to the process.

Alignment of the organization to act on results given by Connects: Any business systems or practices are in-line with the project strategy.

Highly enthusiastic sales engineers looking to grow their territories or segments: Sales engineers act immediately on leads received from Connects and are actively engaged in the process.

Regular participation in meetings with your Connects team: Having an open dialog with the callers assigned to your project. Do you have new products? What are the big wins and losses so far from the leads you've received from us? This communication loop between client and caller is essential in ensuring the best possible results.

Project owner: The client must have someone internally who owns the whole process. This could be the Marketing Manager or someone similar, but this person needs to oversee both the internal and external aspects of the program.

As we are in a B2B world, we all know that the Customer Decision Journey is not short. Clients, particularly the sales engineers, should be measuring success in terms of engagement with target customers. Are you able to connect with the correct targets as a result of your Connects project?

Getting in early on a design, which is often the case, you have to allow time for the design, test, validation and sales cycle to run its course. This means there will be some time before you might see a purchase order.

A sales engineer who is not buying in to a Connects project might say the following:

"I don't want to talk to design engineers. I only want to talk to purchasers."

"I met that person before. She doesn't count as a lead."

"I haven't closed a deal in two weeks. This is not working."

The B2B Customer Decision Journey

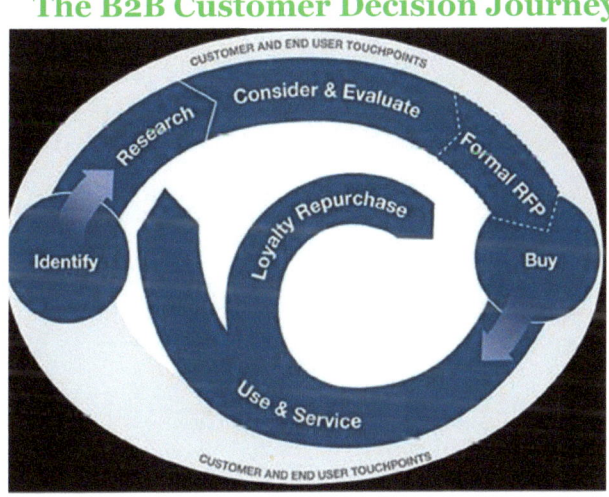

Image Credit: Forbes

The bottom line: Setting yourself up for success with Connects Marketing Group ensures that your will achieve your maximum ROI.

Creating Customers: Building Your Lead Generation Machine

B2B industries are generally more technical and more in-depth than those in the B2C space. We believe that if you can figure out in a B2B world how to give someone a B2C experience, you will own your marketplace. It is our job to help you achieve this goal.

Let's talk about specific projects that create customers.

Lead Generation/Qualification

The heart of what we do is B2B lead generation. We keep your pipeline filled with highly qualified leads so your sales people can spend their time closing deals. Our team has the ability to understand your business and complex technology and then take the right action to ensure your sales success. We begin by:

- Engaging the right point of contact within the targeted company
- Having a candid dialogue that supports future communication
- Identifying true opportunities for your sales team
- Determining the logical next steps for your sales team
- Establishing a firm foundation for a long-term business relationship

Typical types of lead generation campaigns might include:

- New customer creation
- Email or direct mail campaign follow-up
- Territory expansion
- Web-based inquiries
- Trade show registrations or inquiries
- Webinar registration or follow-up
- New product launches

A lead generation project* would look something like this:

- We would **start with a conversation** to discuss your goals and objectives, gain further product/service knowledge etc. and also to share our methodology.

- The client (you) will fill out a **detailed questionnaire.**

- We will develop **an extensive call guide** to be used by the callers assigned to your account. Think of this as their project bible.

- We will build a **database** to include targeted leads and qualifying questions.

- A **call walk-through** will then take place with you.

- Upon approval of all materials, **calling efforts will begin**.

- We attempt to reach prospective leads by placing **three calls** and leaving voicemails. Each attempt is typically followed by an email.

- Upon reaching a live lead, we **deliver our pitch** to determine a current or anticipated need and then qualify that lead as to their level of interest. At the same time, we are always seeking referrals for other prospective leads within the same organization.

- **In-depth details** of our conversations are noted in the database.

- **Leads** showing immediate interest are passed to you for follow-up.

- Other leads are scheduled for **follow-up by Connects** with the goal of moving them up the rating scale at a later date.

- You will receive **reports, feedback and observations** on a daily and weekly basis.

* Each new project begins with the process listed above. In every situation, no matter the type of project, we customize the program to meet your specific goals.

Also, once we are trained on a client's product or service, the process is substantially shortened, since we already know your company, products and services. We use the knowledge already acquired and adjust the focus as needed. This is common for us, as we enjoy long-term relationships with the majority of our clients.

Lead Nurturing and Retention

Not to beat a dead horse, but...

79% of marketing leads never convert into sales. Lack of lead nurturing is the common cause of this poor performance. (*Marketing Sherpa/ KnowledgeStorm*)

One of the most critical aspects of your sales cycle is keeping leads warm until they are ready to purchase. Sales teams don't have time to nurture the pipeline, they need to close deals. Enter your customer creation team. I almost want to call them your nurturing team, because really, all of these core areas are or relate very closely to nurturing.

Your team should keep you connected with your prospects, handing them over when the prospects are ready to take the next step. Your ROI will be maximized and your pipeline kept active with well-paced, ongoing dialog and direct communication.

This means:

- Staying in front of your prospects with new developments and offerings
- Allowing connections to be deepened with relevant decision-makers
- Identifying new sales opportunities
- Maintaining your sales pipeline so it is current and up to date

Appointment Setting

Let's say you have a sales engineer who is going to be traveling in the southeast United States region for a week. While he's there, you want him to make the most of his time. Generally, we do appointment setting for existing clients; therefore we are already well-versed in their products, services and industries. We can certainly do appointment setting for new clients as well.

Imagine breaking into a territory for a new product launch with a full week of qualified appointments. Whether you are looking for face-to-face or phone-based appointments, we can help your sales team keep their calendars full, not just handing over leads for future follow-up, but working directly with your team to coordinate next steps. Many of our clients find that by conducting appointment setting programs they are able to ensure they are:

- Maximizing sales engineers' time while out in the field
- Increasing ROI for sales travel costs
- Leveraging investments in trade shows or conferences

Connects Program

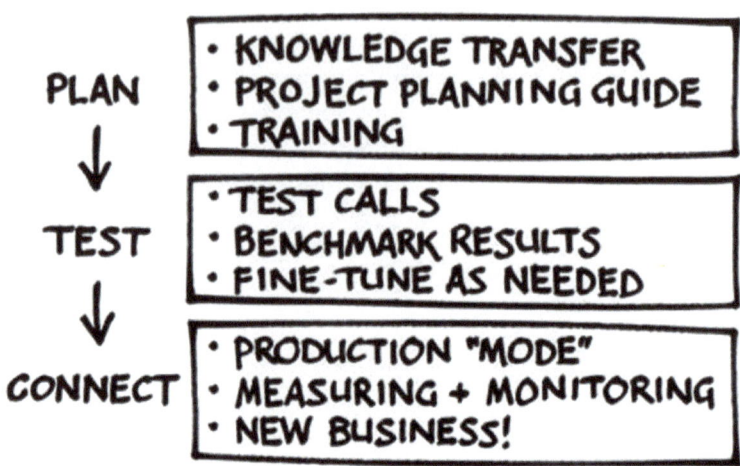

As a part of our integration with our clients, Connects can work within your company's CRM system or calendar to upload reporting information and add appointments. We are well-versed with many platforms, including SalesForce.com, SuperOffice, TimeTrade and many others.

Expanding Customers: Mining the Gold in Your Top Customers

Sometimes the easiest way to increase sales is to leverage your current customers and grow these accounts organically so they meet their full potential. This is especially helpful in your top tier customers. Oftentimes, especially with your larger customers, there are almost always other divisions, other departments or other decision-makers that you don't even know exist. Drilling into these possibilities via account mapping is not only a good idea, it is just common sense.

Below is an excerpt from "Mining the Gold in Existing Customers" via forbes.com, authored by Scott Gillum of gyroVoice.

> *It's conventional wisdom that it is "six to seven times more expensive to gain a new customer than to retain an existing customer." Given today's economic uncertainty, could the inverse also be true? Could existing customers be six, seven or even eight times more valuable in terms of revenue and growth than new ones?*
>
> [Frederick Reichheld](#) *of Bain & Company coined the phrase based on his research on customer retention and acquisition in a study published in the* Harvard Business Review *in 2001. He would later go on to develop the Net Promoter score, measuring the impact and importance of "loyal enthusiasts" on a company's performance.*
>
> *For many companies, existing customers are a bellwether investment, such as gold, in times of instability and uncertainty. But what the research does not address is the potential existing customers represent. Many are a goldmine of opportunity for incremental revenue growth that is often missed.*
>
> *This incremental revenue potential, combined with the value a customer represents as a brand advocate (*[Reichheld's Net Promoter System](#)*) powered by social media raises the stakes*

even further. It is a solid argument for suggesting that existing customers are, in fact, even more valuable than Bain originally suggested 10 years ago.

Let's talk about specific projects that expand your customers.

Account Mapping

Account Mapping is a powerful tool and often gives our clients the greatest ROI. We unearth as many points of contact in one company as possible, piecing together their organization and almost always uncovering potential business of which our clients had no previous knowledge. Connects will work with your sales team to ensure consistent messaging and a powerful strategy for:

- Identifying new contacts and decision-makers
- Discovering new projects and programs
- Understanding the needs of your customers
- Determining the level of satisfaction of your customers with your products and/or services
- Mapping out "the lay of the land;" who does what, where
- Identifying other locations or divisions to replicate success

Account Mapping, along with the customer satisfaction element, give the most significant ROI. Known customers are already set up in all of your business systems. You know all of their purchasing and shipping preferences, etc., so every new piece of business is incrementally profitable.

It's in conversations with these customers that you are likely to get your most valuable information. For example, Customer X will say, "I spend 50 percent of my dollar with you. I'd spend 100% with you if you improved X."

If you make the improvements that these customers note in your general business activities, it's going to help in all of your accounts.

Account Mapping gives you the full lay of the land of your existing accounts. There is an extensive amount of research that goes into these projects, but there is also a wealth of information that is harvested through quality conversation and active listening.

Mapping: It Works!

One of our clients decided to have us map one of its established, top tier customers. The customer, a large aerospace component manufacturer, had a dedicated sales manager who was responsible only for this customer's account.

During the account mapping project with Connects, it was discovered that this customer had a whole sub-division, on the same campus, which our client had never even heard of before.

Our client was able to break into this sub-division, made easier by existing vendor approvals and a proven track record with other parts of the customer's organization, and gain substantial new business.

> Your Existing Customers are Your Biggest Assets

Retaining Customers: Keeping Them Profitable for the Long Term

Retaining customers in today's market means providing exceptional customer service and support. Customers are in complete control and have access to more information than ever before.

Let's talk about specific projects that can help retain customers.

Voice of the Customer (VoC)

VoC is the in-depth process of capturing a customer's expectations, preferences and aversions. However you slice it, VoC means finding out what your customers *really* expect and want from you-- and what they definitely don't. In the simplest of terms, are your customers satisfied? If not, why? How do you fix it?

Gone are the old days and ways of thinking that if you make a great, needed product, customers will come no matter how you treat them. No sir, not in today's digital age. You can be the biggest overnight delivery service in the country, but guess what? You've got smaller, more versatile competitors popping up everywhere, just waiting to gobble up a piece of your pie. You ignore your customers' satisfaction and little by little, you're left staring at your empty plate, fork in hand, thinking, "What happened?!"

Customer satisfaction, the other guys', not yours, is what happened. Those agile up-and-comers swooped right in, and by using VoC like pros, took your market share right out from under you. Are you paying attention yet?

Keeping the lines of communication open with you customers is a crucial aspect of business development. We can help you with this process by implementing a campaign that ensures you are getting reliable feedback from your customers. By gauging the overall satisfaction of your clients, you will gain:

- Insight into the wants and needs of your customers
- Measure the success of your sales and service teams
- Improve on your current processes and initiatives
- Drive future product development

Competitive Analysis

Knowing your competition is as important as understanding the end-users of your products and services. We can help you develop a better picture of the competitive landscape within your markets. This will not only entail identifying the key players who share your space but also getting a better idea of how compare to your product offerings. From this you gain powerful insight and are able to:

- Develop a competitive matrix of key products and benefits
- Understand competitors' strengths and weaknesses
- Refine your branding and messaging

Market Research

We understand that business does not happen in a static space or a vacuum; it's dynamic and always changing. That is why we feel it is important that research be a part of any marketing program. By periodically researching your markets you will be able to:

- Understand market dynamics and trends to help develop ongoing strategies
- Support product development by determining what the market needs
- Measure the size and growth rates of markets
- Understand new verticals before you start selling or marketing to them

In all of our projects, we strive to get referrals and grow our clients' databases.

Other Core Competencies: Tools to Make Your Business Hum

With core competencies spanning the entire business life cycle, we offer a breadth of solutions with deep expertise in each area. After an initial needs assessment, we can help you pinpoint your key areas of pain and develop a strategy to streamline operations, drive revenue and reduce costs regardless of where you are in your planning, execution or measurement processes.

Executive and Business Strategy: With more than 36 years of global manufacturing experience— including 10 in the position of president of the American arm of an international corporation—our senior business strategist helps clients implement:

- Policy deployment
- Growth initiatives
- Segment management
- Talent management
- Acquisition support
- Project management culture
- Accelerated innovation initiatives

Marketing Communications and Public Relations: Our team of consultants can shape your ideas into stories and help you share your stories with the world. Experienced in multiple industries, from banking to industrial manufacturing, they also have their fingers on the pulse of emerging online and social media channels to help with your:

- PR framework
- Copywriting and copy editing
- Media relations
- Value proposition messaging and positioning
- Promotion
- Newsroom optimization

Sales Onboarding and Readiness: Our solution sales experts have developed training, sales tools and strategic playbooks for sales teams and partners of the world's largest technology companies, including:

- Classroom and online training courses for role readiness, product launches and solution selling
- Internal sales tools and readiness materials
- Sales scripts and role plays
- Customer-facing presentations

Innovation Training: Connects Innovation is our cross-consulting group with experts ranging from executive-level business developers to global sales and marketing consultants, working in collaboration with SolutionPeople® Innovation Acceleration tools and methodology to provide customized innovation workshops for individuals and organizations that want to grow through innovation. We lead Accelerating Innovation and Creativity Training workshops to help clients develop innovative solutions for:

- Annual business planning at the executive level
- Measurement metrics and performance indicators to evaluate successful execution against business plans
- Market campaign messaging, positioning and definition
- Competitive positioning in a rapidly changing marketplace
- Quarterly or annual review of business and team performance and definition of corrections of error to improve success in the coming term

- Innovative internal process improvements for increased customer satisfaction
- Product repositioning or launches
- Product/service development

Reporting: The Feedback Loop to Refine Your Efforts

Real-time reporting is a key element of the Connects program. It provides a continual feedback loop, and we believe this information is invaluable to our clients. It also allows us to adjust your program to be most effective.

Depending on the type of project, reports will vary. Reports can be given in almost any requested format and the data we capture can be presented by any metrics you wish to highlight.

What You Will Receive

At Start-Up	Daily	Weekly
✦ Initial questionnaire to handle knowledge transfer	✦ Highly qualified leads as they are developed	✦ Detailed statistics and reporting
✦ Project planning guide used for training	✦ Feedback on how the program is running	✦ List of all connections from the prior week
✦ Two dedicated callers for your program	✦ Quick snapshot reports detailing latest results	✦ Observations and recommendations for the project
✦ One project manager who will oversee your success		

Report Example #1

Week in Review
6/17/2013 – 6/23/2013

Hours	Calls	CPH	Pres.	PPH	Pres.%	Opps	Opps %	Cost
25.25	184	7.29	58	2.30	31.5%	5	8.6%	$277.75

Hot	Warm	Pending	Lit Only	No Interest	Referral	Bad
5	5	9	0	9	19	2
8.6%	8.6%	15.5%	0%	15.5%	32.8%	N/A

Comments: We were successful at uncovering 5 new opportunities last week, 14 contacts requested further follow up, 9 had no interest and we added 19 new referrals into Salesforce.

Report Example #2

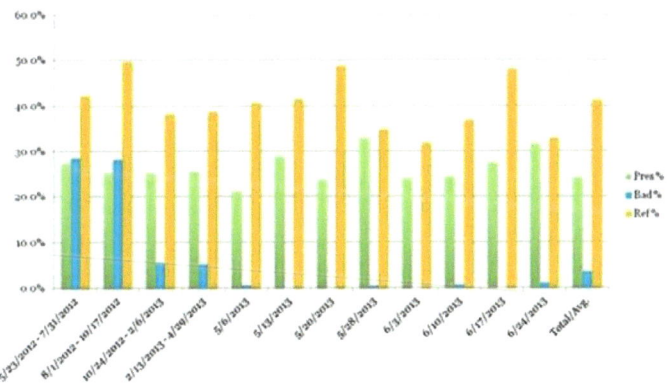

Case Studies: How It Works in the Real World

Study #1

Client: Medium-sized Software Company with a four-person inside sales team

Company provides identity management solutions designed to improve security and operational efficiencies and help achieve regulatory compliance.

Project Focus: We started working with this client when they had just opened their doors. We did all of the front-end work to fill their sales pipeline.

After seven years, in reviewing their sales history, the client stated that 100% of their sales stemmed from the work that Connects performed.

This client's end goal was to grow large enough to be acquired, and they accomplished that goal.

Example ROI

Results for the period:

Hours budgeted:		16.00	
Hours completed:		16.00	
Hours remaining:		00.00	
Calling hours completed:	11.50	Other hours completed:	4.50
Total calls:	86	Calls per hour:	7.48
Total e-mails:	79	E-mails per hour:	6.87
Total presentations:	8	Presentations per hour:	.70
Discovery Calls / Demos Scheduled:	4	Discovery / Demo Conversion:	50.0%
Presentation/Call Ratio:	9.3%	Disc. & Demo/Call Ratio:	4.7%
Cost per Discovery / Demo:	$220		

Study #2

Client: Global medical device manufacturer

Company has an extremely successful brand name in the consumer market.

Project Focus: Connects assisted this client in expanding into its underserved segment of hospitals and surgery centers with large-area decontamination and sterilization equipment.

Client originally had seven sales representatives responsible for the product line being promoted, but due to attrition the number was reduced to five.

The two Connects project managers assigned to this project virtually became the client's inside sales department, becoming personally invested in seeing the remaining sales reps succeed.

Again, 100% of sales for this division stemmed from work Connects did.

Sample ROI

Results for the period:

Hours budgeted:	94.50
Hours completed:	83.00
Hours remaining:	10.50

Calling hours completed:	81.25	Other hours completed:	1.75
Total calls	1166	Calls per hour:	14.35
Total presentations:	214	Presentations per hour:	2.63
Qualified Leads:	22	Qualification Percentage:	**10.3%**
Pending Leads:	31	Pending Percentage:	14.5%
No Interest:	92	No Interest Percentage:	43.0%
Cost per Qualified Lead:	$207		

Study #3

Client: Global seal manufacturer

Company engineers and manufactures sealing solutions for the industrial marketplace.

Project Focus: Connects worked with this client for several years. The ROI and Scalability reports below are a compilation of results from over 100 projects over the span of one year, including lead generation, nurturing, appointment setting and mapping, etc.

Sample ROI

Results for the period: 2012
Hours budgeted: 8998
Hours completed: 8998
Hours remaining: 0

Calling hours completed:	6,636	Other hours completed:	2,362
Total calls:	91,577	Calls per hour:	13.18
Total e-mails:	12,343	E-mails per hour:	1.86
Total presentations:	15,130	Presentations per hour:	2.28
Appointments Scheduled:	2,269	Appointment Conversion:	15%
Presentation/Call Ratio:	17%		
Cost per Appointment:	$235		

Testimonials: What Our Clients Think

"Connects Marketing Group has exceeded my expectations. The quality of their employees is unparalleled. They have learned our business and pivot quickly offering us valuable feedback from our customers and prospects. The effectiveness of our campaigns came from Connects taking the initiative to learn our industry, when we did not have the time to train them. They are an integral part of our sales process. I highly recommend them."

Roger Parks,
VP Business Development & Co-Founder
doxo, Inc.

"The people at Connects Marketing Group offered us an uncommon perspective in both design and execution of a business development program. And they truly delivered quality leads to pursue that resulted in new business opportunities that connected back to revenue for our company."

Jason Fradin
VP Marketing
Infologix

"CMG as a partner is tenacious and always deliver what they promise. They can take a complex concept or sale, break it down methodically, and have a targeted message to share with the prospective customer while speaking the party line of our company. Working with CMG gives us the ability to turn up or dial down activity in a program offering without additional sales and marketing costs being incurred. We've utilized them for lead generation and are pleased they offer so many additional relevant B2B Business Development services. We see them as an extension our on-staff sales teams.
"CMG's greatest strength is their smart and highly engaged people and how quickly they get a sales management program

launched. It takes a special breed of people to pick up the phone and clearly communicate the marketing message. If you are going to spend money on a tradeshow, you have to take advantage of the leads and do the follow up. The best way to get ROI of any tradeshow is to utilize Connects. Within a day or two they will literally touch every lead received from a tradeshow. CMG leaves no stone unturned and that is key in turning prospects into customers efficiently and quickly."

Jeff Heier
Security Solutions Strategist
CA Technologies

Conclusion

Quality conversations, active listening, compassion and the human element are vitally important in creating, expanding and retaining customers. We have found that, above anything else, people just want to be HEARD.

It sounds simple enough, but, if so, then why aren't more companies doing it?

Connects Marketing Group has a genuine, vested interest in our clients and their customers. We want you to succeed.

Each and every one of our callers and project managers is dedicated to your success!

Helpful Resources: Industry-Leading Blogs

- www.b2bknowledgesharing.com
- blog.hubspot.com
- www.b2bmarketinginsider.com
- blog.eloqua.com
- sherpablog.marketingsherpa.com
- www.forbes.com/cmo-network
- contentmarketinginstitute.com
- b2bleadblog.com
- thesalesblog.com
- blogs.salesforce.com/company

About the Author

Robin Black

Robin Black brings her extensive sales and marketing project management skills to the forefront when supporting her clients. With over 20 years of experience in sales and marketing, account management and customer relations, Robin always looks forward to the new challenges that new projects bring.

At Connects Marketing Group, Robin and her team develop new business opportunities and highly qualified leads for their clients. They open doors so you can close deals.

Robin possesses a professional and effervescent personality; she is a believer in clear communication, a deep respect for best practices and continuous process improvement. After a lifetime in sales, she knows the importance of quality leads. She knows sales people must be efficient with their time by talking to decision-makers and closing deals. She founded Connects to help clients find the services, solutions and resources that will lead to exponential sales growth.

In her previous positions, Robin was a principal at a lead generation firm and prior to that she was a field sales manager for eight years at an electronics manufacturers' representative agency. Robin has in-depth knowledge of the high tech, medical instrumentation, industrial and computer markets.

Robin's bottom line? **Connections Matter.**

www.ingramcontent.com/pod-product-compliance
Lightning Source LLC
Chambersburg PA
CBHW040833180526
45159CB00001B/167